put on a

happy face

Library of Congress Cataloging-in-Publication Data available.

ISBN 0-8118-4042-5

Manufactured in China.

Designed by Iza Dar

Distributed in Canada by Raincoast Books
9050 Shaughnessy Street
Vancouver, British Columbia V6P 6E5

10 9 8 7 6 5 4 3 2 1

Chronicle Books LLC
85 Second Street
San Francisco, California 94105
www.chroniclebooks.com

put on a
happy face

a book of smiles, happiness, and joy

Cooper Edens and Richard Kehl

CHRONICLE BOOKS

SAN FRANCISCO

Be happy.

It's one way of being wise.

—Colette

Grab your coat, and get your hat,

Leave your worry on the doorstep,

Just direct your feet,

To the sunny side of the street.

—Fields and McHugh

When you're smiling,

when you're smiling,

The whole world smiles with you.

—Fisher, Goodwin, and Shay

Says yes when nobody asks.

—Lao proverb

Twice I have lived forever in a smile.

—e.e. cummings

Deserve your dream.

—Octavio Paz

Happy trails to you, until we meet again.
Happy trails to you, keep smilin' until then.

—Dale Evans

Happy new now.

—John Lennon

I dwell in possibility.

—Emily Dickinson

Happiness is not an elusive bird.
Happiness is an element,
Which, like air, is everywhere.

—Jacques-Henri Lartigue

Hallelujah anyhow!

—Kenneth Patchen

We believe as much as we can.
We would believe everything if we could.

—William James

Grey skies are going to clear up…
just put on a happy face.

—Adams and Strouse

I sing, I sing,

from morning till night;

From cares I'm free,

and my heart is light.

—Mother Goose

And now I have to confess the
unpardonable and the scandalous. I
am a happy man. **And I am going to tell
you the secret of my happiness.**
It is quite simple. I love mankind. I love love.
I hate hate. I try to understand and accept.

—Jean Cocteau

Everyone

is indispensable.

—Colette

CREDITS

Front endpapers: Beach Beauties, tinted postcard, Genuine Curteich, Chicago, n.d. **Front inside endpaper:** illustration from *More Jumbo Stories* by Harry Neilson, n.d. **p. 4** English bow tie display poster, circa 1926 **p. 6** Cunard White Star Cruise Poster, circa 1920 **p. 7** toy robot, collage by Cooper Edens, 1960s **p. 8** illustration from *Tuffy the Truck*, illustrator unknown, Jolly Books, circa 1950s **p. 9** monkey god and Krishnu, East Indian lithographic print, n.d. **p. 10** "Girl of Mine" sheet music, illustration by Holt Armstrong, 1917 **p. 11** anonymous studio portrait, n.d. **p. 12** Kodak magazine ad, circa 1920s **p. 13** *Spring*, Giuseppe Arcimboldo, 1573 **p. 14** illustration from *The Roosevelt Bears Abroad*, R.K. Culver, circa 1905 **p. 15** lyrics from "The Sunny Side of the Street" by Dorothy Fields and Jimmy McHugh, 1930 **p. 16** English postcard, circa 1900 **p. 17** anonymous photograph, 1950s **p. 18** German circus handbill, Ausstellungs Park, 1860–1880 **p. 19** "A Little Visitor in Space," Chinese poster, 1980 **p. 20** *Woman with Lantern*, Chica Y. Ulpina, London, n.d. **p. 21** "The Girls of the Golden West," Dolly and Milly Good, circa 1930s **p. 22** German Halloween candy container, 1920s–1930s **p. 23** June Allison, Goodyear Tires magazine ad, 1940s **p. 24** anonymous calendar art, circa 1930s **p. 25** anonymous Japanese magazine ad, n.d. **p. 26** Cooper Edens, age 7, Rainer Beach, Washington, 1952 **p. 27** Marilyn Monroe, photo by Andre de Dienes, Tobey Beach New York, 1949. Reprinted by permission of C.M.G. Worldwide, Indianapolis, Indiana. **p. 28** Hopalong Cassidy puzzle, 1950 **p. 29** lyrics from "When You're Smiling" by Joe Goodwin, Mark Fisher, and Larry Shay, 1928 **p. 30** Japanese ceramic Buddha coin bank, n.d. **p. 31** Kellogg's Toasted Corn Flakes ad, 1917 **p. 32** anonymous Mexican calendar art, n.d. **p. 33** collage by Richard Kehl, 1990 **p. 34** Josephine Baker, photograph by Piaz, Paris, circa 1930 **p. 35** ink drawing, Henri Matisse, 1950s **p. 36** *A Girl and Her Duenna*, Bartolome Esteban Murillo, 1670 **p. 37** tin monkey toy, photograph by Ian Hessenberg, 1960s **p. 38** *Marimba Lesson 2*, record sleeve, circa 1950s **p. 39** altered photograph of Albert Einstein, n.d. Reprinted by permission of The Roger Richman Agency, Beverly Hills, California. **p. 40** lyrics from "Happy Trails" by Dale Evans, 1950 **p. 41** lyrics from "Put on a Happy Face" by Lee Adams and Charles Strouse, 1960 **p. 42** anonymous postcard, 1950s **p. 43** Quaker Oats Man, 1900s. The Quaker Oats Man is the registered trademark for the Quaker Oats Company, Chicago, Illinois. **p. 44** Froggy the Gremlin, rubber toy from the *Smiling Ed* television show, 1950s **p. 45** "Aix-les-Bains," poster, Cappiello, 1921 **p. 46** Barbara Ogden, 5 years old, West Seattle, Washington, 1952 **p. 47** English rag doll, 1930 **p. 48** illustration from *Dick Tracy Solves the Penfield Mystery*, Chester Gould, 1934 **p. 49** anonymous fruit crate art, n.d. **p. 50** Richard Kehl, 5 years old, Mexico, Missouri, 1941 **p. 51** ad for Brer Rabbit molasses, 1931 **p. 52** illustration from *Mother Goose's Menageries*, Peter Newell, 1901 **p. 54** Valentine's Day card, circa 1955 **p. 55** *Mona Lisa*, Italian photolitho postcard, circa 1910 **p. 56** anonymous American print, n.d. **p. 57** Hagenbeck-Wallace circus poster, 1929 **p. 58** anonymous illustration from *Bubbles and Friends*, circa 1900 **p. 59** Humphrey Bogart, circa 1954. Reprinted by permission of Quantity Postcards, Oakland, California. **p. 60** "Gracia–Princess de Monaco," Carte Postale, Imp. Moderne de Biarritz, n.d. **p. 61** paper insert for cardboard jack-o'-lantern, early 1950s **p. 62** Mego Man, photograph by Masashi Kudo, 1960s **p. 63** Herman Munster, circa 1960s. Reprinted by permission of Pyramid Postcards, Leicester, England. **p. 64** Rimini poster, A. Busi, 1929 **p. 65** Willie Mays baseball card, 1955 **p. 66** Black Cat hosiery display, 1907 **p. 68** calendar art, Gene Pressler, 1925 **p. 69** "Tip to Tip," German photolitho postcard, pre-1905 **p. 70** English print, Frances Tipton Hunter, n.d. **p. 71** Mr. Peanut, cloth doll, 1904 **p. 72** magazine ad, Gustaf Tenggren, n.d. **p. 73** "A Pair of Suspenders," postcard, 1913 **p. 74** Stan Laurel, French postcard, n.d. **p. 75** "Hard Work Nurtures Fragrant Flowers," Chinese poster, 1962 **p. 76** Kewpie doll, anonymous photograph, n.d. **p. 78** tinted Italian postcard, late 1920s **p. 80** Alice and the Cheshire Cat, illustration by John Tenniel, 1890 **Back inside end-paper:** magazine cover, Hyman W. Pertweig, circa 1920 **Back endpapers:** anonymous Victorian illustration, circa 1900